Life Cycles

Silkworms

by Donna Schaffer

Consultant:
Richard Mankin, Ph.D.
USDA—Agricultural Research Service
Center for Medical, Agricultural,
and Veterinary Entomology

Bridgestone Books
an imprint of Capstone Press
Mankato, Minnesota

Bridgestone Books are published by Capstone Press
151 Good Counsel Drive, P.O. Box 669, Mankato, Minnesota 56002
http://www.capstone-press.com

Library of Congress Cataloging-in-Publication Data
Schaffer, Donna.
   Silkworms/by Donna Schaffer.
     p. cm.—(Life cycles)
   Includes bibliographical references (p. 23) and index.
   Summary: Describes the physical characteristics, habits, and stages of development
of silkworms, as well as how they are raised to produce silk.
     ISBN 0-7368-0213-4
     1. Silkworms—Life cycles—Juvenile literature. [1. Silkworms.] I. Title. II. Series:
Schaffer, Donna. Life cycles.
QL561.B6S36   1999
595.78—dc21
                                                                              98-53030
                                                                                    CIP
                                                                                     AC

Editorial Credits
Christy Steele, editor; Steve Weil/Tandem Design, cover designer; Linda Clavel,
   illustrator; Kimberly Danger, photo researcher

Photo Credits
David Liebman, 6
Dwight R. Kuhn, 8
Em Ahart, 10 (inset), 12-13, 16, 18 (inset)
Michael Ventura, 10
Robert and Linda Mitchell, 4
Visuals Unlimited, 14; Visuals Unlimited/Ken Lucas, cover; John D. Cunningham, 18;
Steve McCutcheon, 20

3 4 5 6 04 03 02

Table of Contents

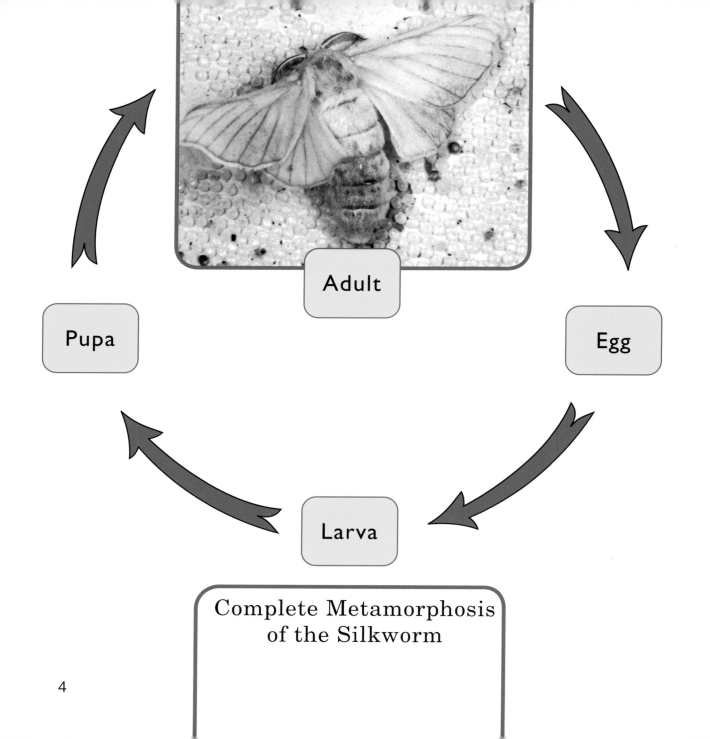

Pupa

Adult

Egg

Larva

Complete Metamorphosis
of the Silkworm

The Life Cycle of Silkworms

Silkworms go through complete metamorphosis. Complete metamorphosis has four stages. Silkworms grow and change during each stage. A silkworm's body changes form four times.

The first stage is the egg. Silkworms grow in eggs during this stage. Larvas hatch from eggs. Silkworms are larvas during the second life stage. Larvas spin cocoons around their bodies to become pupas. During this third stage, pupas grow adult body parts. Finally, the pupa becomes an adult moth.

These stages are part of a silkworm's life cycle. Almost all living things go through this cycle of birth, growth, reproduction, and death.

About Silkworms

Silkworm is the common name for several kinds of moths. Farmers collect the valuable silk these insects spin. People make expensive clothes from silk.

Silkworms live mainly in Asia. Some silkworms live in the wild. But most silkworms are domesticated. People raise them on farms.

Silkworm moths share some features with all insects. The silkworm moth has three main body parts. They are the head, thorax, and abdomen. Silkworm moths smell with antennas attached to the head. Wings are attached to the thorax. The stomach is in the abdomen.

Silkworm moths use their long, featherlike antennas to smell.

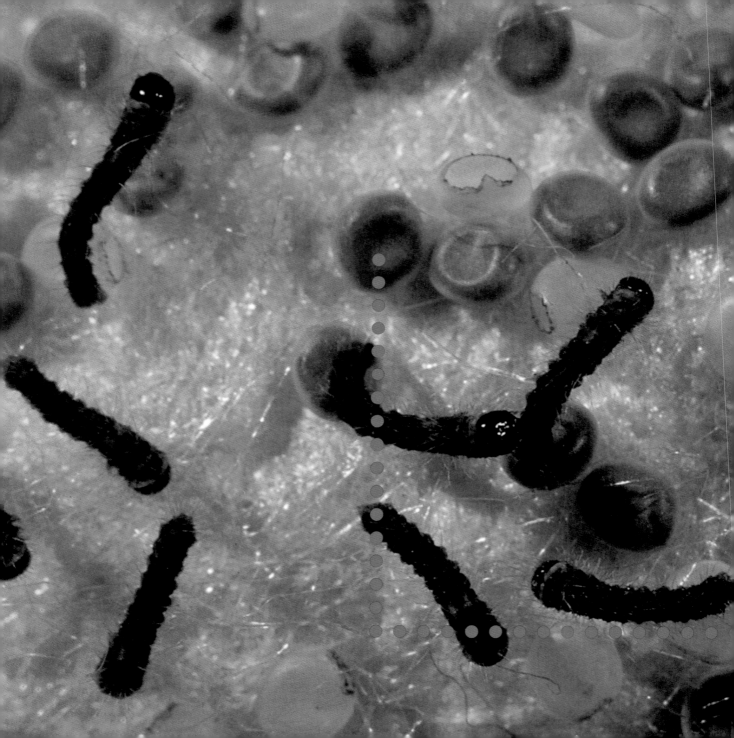

The Life Cycle Begins

The life of a silkworm begins in an egg. A female silkworm moth lays 300 to 400 yellow eggs at one time. A special body part in her abdomen releases the eggs.

In the wild, silkworm moths lay eggs mainly on mulberry leaves. The moth releases a sticky liquid that fastens the eggs to plant surfaces. This keeps the eggs from falling or being eaten easily by predators.

Not all eggs hatch. Eggs that will hatch turn black within three days. Silkworms in the black eggs develop for seven to 20 days. They may develop more quickly in warm conditions. Over time, the egg centers become clear. Eggs are ready to hatch when black rings appear in the center.

The black rings are larvas. The larvas hatch by eating their way out of the eggs. The second life stage of the silkworm begins.

● ● ● ● **Silkworms hatch from black eggs. White eggs will not hatch.**

Larvas

People named the silkworm for the way it looks in the larval stage. Newly hatched larvas look like thin worms.

Larvas must eat within 24 hours after they hatch. Newly hatched larvas are weak after they break out of their eggs. They do not have much energy to move around to find food.

Silkworm larvas begin eating mulberry leaves right after they hatch. They first eat the leaf on which they hatched. Larvas continue to eat and grow. Farmers feed mulberry leaves to domesticated silkworms.

Larvas have hard outer coverings called exoskeletons. Exoskeletons protect larvas. Birds and other predators cannot easily break through the exoskeleton.

● ● ● ● **These larvas are eating mulberry leaves. Larvas are in the eating and growing stage of the life cycle. The larva in the circle is older than the other larvas. It has grown larger.**

Molting

Silkworm larvas must shed their exoskeletons to grow. This process is called molting.

Larvas must molt four times before entering the next life stage. A silkworm larva stops eating when it is ready to molt. It then raises its head and keeps still. The larva stays this way for about one day.

The larva produces a liquid to loosen its exoskeleton. The larva then crawls out of its old covering. The new covering is softer and larger. The larva begins to eat again. It will grow into its new covering. The larva is ready to molt again when the covering becomes tight and hard.

Scientists call the stage between each molt an instar. Silkworms have five instars. Larvas have different coloring during each instar. Silkworms reach the final instar in about two weeks.

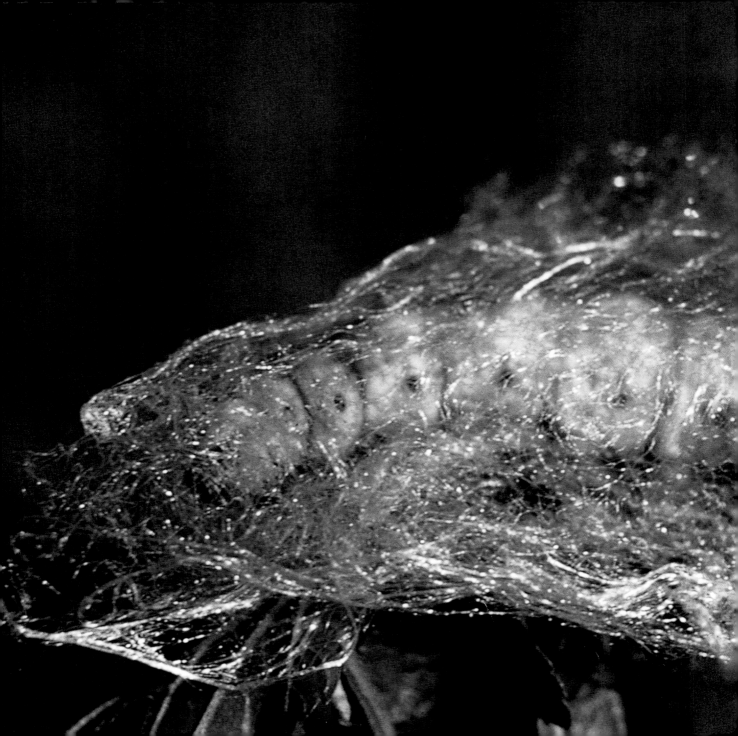

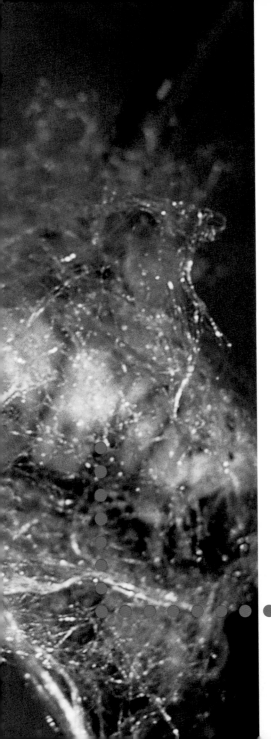

The Fifth Instar

Silkworm larvas spend about eight days in the fifth instar. They eat and grow the most during this time.

Larvas need food to use as energy during their next life stage. After the fifth instar, silkworms will weigh 10,000 times more than when they first hatched.

Silk glands make up about one-fourth of the larva's weight. These body parts release liquid that hardens into strings of silk.

Before moving to the next life stage, the larva stops eating. It hangs upside down and uses its silk to make a cocoon. The larva spins a silk string around itself to make its cocoon.

It may take this silkworm up to one month to finish its cocoon. One silk thread may be one-half mile (.8 kilometer) long.

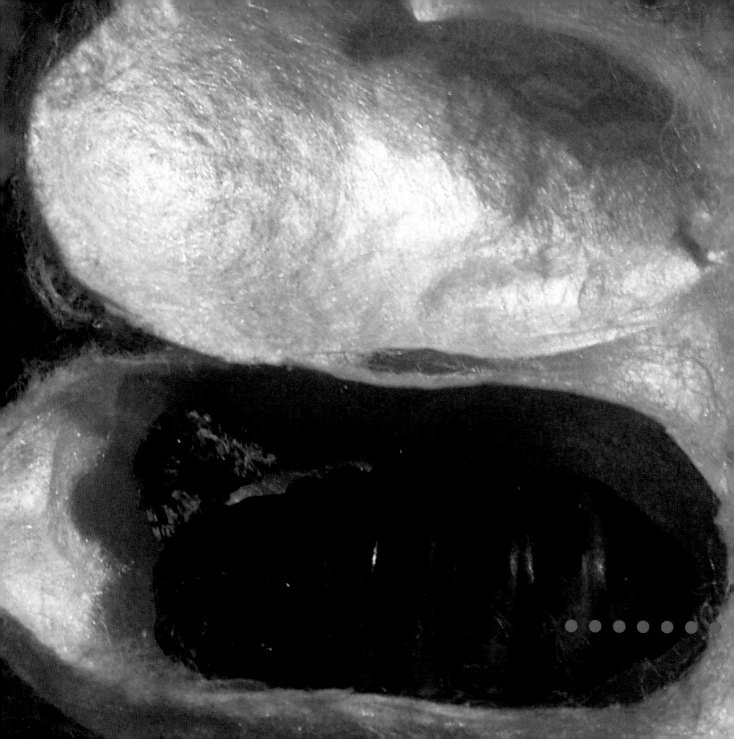

Pupas

Larvas become pupas when they are inside cocoons. Larvas molt one final time before entering this third life stage.

Pupas have hard, brown shells. The shells protect pupas as they change and grow. Pupas become moths inside these shells.

Pupas do not move. They use all their energy to change and grow. Scaly wings form. Long, jointed legs grow. Antennas and large eyes form. The mouthparts also change.

Silkworms stay in the pupal stage for about three weeks. The adult moths then are ready to break out of their shells.

● ● ● ● ● **The pupa is inside its cocoon. Beside the pupa is the exoskeleton it shed during its last molt.**

Adult Silkworm Moths

The pupa's brown shell splits open when the silkworm moth is fully grown. The silkworm then begins its fourth and final life stage.

The adult pushes its way out of the pupal shell. But it still has to free itself from the silk cocoon. Silk is very strong. The adult releases a special liquid to dissolve the silk.

Silkworm moths have heavy bodies and short wings. They cannot fly. Male moths are smaller than female moths.

An adult silkworm's only purpose is to mate to continue the life cycle. The adult does not even eat or drink. Females release a special scent to help males find them. A male and a female mate for one day. The male then finds another female to mate with. Females lay eggs.

Adult silkworm moths die within five days. But the life cycle will begin again with the eggs.

● ● ● ● **This silkworm moth has pushed its way out of its cocoon. The moth is now ready to mate.**

People and Silkworms

Farmers have bred silkworms for thousands of years. They have allowed only silkworms with certain features to mate. Silkworms once had long wings and were able to fly. Today, farmers allow only silkworms with short wings to mate. Silkworms that do not fly are easier to raise.

Silkworms once made yellow silk. Today, farmers breed silkworms that make white silk. White silk can be dyed different colors.

To make silk, workers boil the cocoons when silkworms are at the pupal stage. This process kills the pupas before they become adults. Otherwise, the adults would break through the cocoons and damage the silk threads. Workers then unwind the silk from cocoons.

Farmers sell the silk threads. People make scarves, ties, and other clothing from silk.

● ● ● ● **Workers sort cocoons. Next, they will unwind silk from the cocoons.**

Hands On: Cocoon Game

Adult silkworms work very hard to break out of their strong cocoons. You can play this game to see how strong cocoons are.

What You Need
String
A friend

What You Do
1. Make a fist with your hand. Have your friend wrap string around your fist. Do not wrap the string too tightly. Your fist should be completely wrapped with string.
2. Wrap string completely around your friend's fist. You have made cocoons like silkworm larvas do.
3. You and your friend should put your free hand behind your back.
4. Move the fingers of your cocooned hand. Use your fingers to break out of the cocoon.
5. The first person to break out of the cocoon wins.

Words to Know

cocoon (kuh-KOON)—a covering made from silky threads; silkworms make cocoons to protect themselves during the pupal stage.

exoskeleton (eks-oh-SKEL-uht-uhn)—a hard, bony covering on the outside of an animal

instar (IN-star)—a stage between molts in the life cycle of certain insects

life cycle (LIFE SYE-kuhl)—the series of changes a living thing goes through

metamorphosis (met-uh-MOR-fuh-siss)—the changes some animals go through as they develop from eggs to adults

molt (MOHLT)—to shed an outer covering so that a new one can grow

Read More

Feltwell, John. *Butterflies and Moths.* Eyewitness Explorers. New York: DK Publishing, 1997.

Opler, Paul A. *Peterson First Guide to Butterflies and Moths.* Boston: Houghton Mifflin, 1994.

Useful Addresses

Department of Entomology
Royal Ontario Museum
Toronto, ON M5S 2C6
Canada

Young Entomologists'
   Society
6907 West Grand River
   Avenue
Lansing, MI 48906

Internet Sites

Cecropia Moth—Life Cycle
http://www.geocities.com/RainForest/5479/index.html
Making Silk
http://www.cambodia.org/clubs/khemara/mulberry.htm

Index